Soul of Tokyo

A GUIDE TO EXCEPTIONAL EXPERIENCES

WRITTEN BY FANY AND AMANDINE PÉCHIODAT
CO-WRITTEN BY IWONKA BANCEREK
ILLUSTRATED BY KANAKO KUNO

JONGLEZ PUBLISHING
Travel guides

鰹
鰊
鯛

‘JAPAN TASTES
LIKE A GRAIN
OF RICE.

YOU HAVE TO BITE
INTO IT *GENTLY*.

AND GET
TO ITS HEART.’

FRANÇOIS SIMON

WHAT YOU WON'T FIND IN THIS GUIDE

- 'Tokyo 101' from the city's tourist office
- the Japanese translation of 'buy a subway ticket'
- what medications to bring

WHAT YOU WILL FIND IN THIS GUIDE

- the ultimate cocktail
- a secret restaurant in Shibuya
- a teahouse hidden behind a flower shop
- the wildest onsen
- the best head massage
- the world's smallest bookstore
- the Japanese translation of 'taking a forest bath'

SYMBOLS USED IN **SOUL OF TOKYO**

< 40 euros

40 to 80 euros

> 80 euros

They don't speak English here, so ask your hotel (or a Japanese friend) to make a reservation

100% traditional Japanese

Even better for couples

You'll often find yourself needing to show your taxi driver the addresses in this guide, so we've included them in Japanese on each page

---

Opening times often vary,
so we recommend checking them directly
on the website of the place you plan to visit.

HOW THIS GUIDE **WORKS**

A CITY PUT UNDER THE MICROSCOPE

+

QUIRKY ENCOUNTERS

(with a tea master, creator of emotions, Michelin-starred chef/son of a geisha)

+

HUNDREDS OF PLACES TESTED

−

OVER-EXPOSED PLACES REJECTED

+

UNCHARTED SPOTS SNIFFED OUT

+

HUNDREDS OF PIECES OF SUSHI DEVOURED

+

GALLONS OF GREEN TEA SIPPED

+

A TOKYO-BORN-AND-BRED ILLUSTRATOR

+

MILES OF STREETS ROAMED

−

A FEW DEAD ENDS

=

The best 30 places in Tokyo

30 EXPERIENCES

1. Drink the ultimate cocktail
2. A teahouse amidst the flowers
3. Tokyo's best concept store
4. A hidden restaurant in Shibuya
5. Spend a night on a library bookshelf
6. François Simon's favorite sushi place
7. A traditional Japanese bath surrounded by plants
8. The Michelin-starred chef who does things like no one else
9. One thousand two hundred and thirty-three shades of paper
10. Have lunch in a Japanese garden
11. The world's biggest bookstore
12. The world's smallest bookstore
13. Magic, pure and simple
14. Celebrate your 'un-birthday'
15. A timeless music bar
16. Have dinner at the old folks'
17. Go on a bike ride in Tokyo
18. Drink yuzu juice at the Nezu Museum
19. Mini-street, maxi-bender
20. A break from the hustle and bustle of city life
21. Spend a few hours in a love hotel
22. Spend a night in old Tokyo
23. Listen to classical music in a bar from the 1950s
24. Treat yourself to a head spa
25. 'Apply' to a restaurant
26. Eat the best sandwich of your life
27. Eat art
28. Spend a magical night outside of town
29. Stay at a capsule hotel
30. The craziest museum

7
17
22
24
新宿
Shinjuku
千代田
Chiyoda
29
20
8
18
4
6
2
15
港
Minato
13
12
9
1
10
26
東京
TOKYO
Kanako
品川
Shinagawa
30

#01

DRINK THE **ULTIMATE COCKTAIL**

When you sip a cocktail at Gen Yamamoto, you'll feel like it's the first time you've ever had a real one.

Sit in monastic silence on one of only eight seats at this tiny bar and witness a unique mixology ceremony: a subtle procession of meticulous gestures, during which Yamamoto slices a yuzu with religious devotion, disrobes a tomato, and metes out gin and sake with the precision of a mad scientist.

Mandarin, milk vodka, and Japanese beans. Kiwi and Normandy gin. Passion fruit and whisky. In the form of six cocktails, you'll discover stunning combinations in a glass, as unexpected as they are memorable.

GEN YAMAMOTO
1-6-4 AZABU-JUBAN, MINATO-KU,
ANNIVERSARY BUILDING 1F

東京都港区麻布十番1-6-4
アニバーサリービル1F

Reservation by e-mail required
office@genyamamoto.jp
genyamamoto.jp
+81 3-6434-0652

4 cocktails: 5,500 yen
6 cocktails: 7,500 yen

#02

A TEA HOUSE **AMIDST THE FLOWERS**

At first glance, it looks like a nice little neighborhood flower shop. But hidden away behind the bouquets, in a greenhouse overflowing with flowers, you'll find a teahouse that's pure zen. Waitresses wearing cloth florist's aprons dispense teapots brimming with herbal brews made from herbs cut fresh that morning. Stop here to catch your breath before or after a hectic run around town.

AOYAMA FLOWER MARKET TEA HOUSE
5-1-2 MINAMI-AOYAMA, MINATO-KU

東京都港区南青山5-1-2

Reservation recommended
+81 3-3400-0887

afm-teahouse.com/aoyama

AOYAMA FLOWER MARKET TEA HOUSE

AOYAMA
FLOWER
MARKET
TEA HOUSE
AOYAMA
FLOWERMARKET
TEA
TEA
HOUSE
HOUSE

#03

TOKYO'S BEST **CONCEPT STORE**

Call (a contraction of 'creation' and 'all'), which opened a year ago in the Omotesando district, feels like a cheerful house where three generations work side-by-side: the youngest saleswoman is 20 years old, the oldest 83. Minä likes mixing generations in all her spaces and often hires retirees who aren't ready to stop working. At Call, as you stroll from room to room, you'll discover a grocery story, a restaurant with a patio on stilts, and a textile workshop.

CALL
(Enter through the Spiral store, then take the elevator on the left to 5th floor)
5-6-23 MINAMI-AOYAMA, MINATO-KU, SPIRAL, 5th FLOOR

東京都港区南青山5-6-23
SPIRAL5階

+81 3-6825-3733

mp-call.jp

CALL

#04

A HIDDEN RESTAURANT **IN SHIBUYA**

They say that hopeless romantics fall in love three times a day. In Yuri Nomura's case, it happens with every meal. Her greatest love affair is with food. After studying in England and cutting her culinary teeth in the kitchens of Paris and San Francisco (at Alice Waters' famous flagship, Chez Panisse), she came back to Japan and opened Eatrip, a small oasis of green, hidden away in the chaos of Shibuya.

Under a skylight, on large wooden tables, she serves up simple dishes, colorful and suffused with sweetness, made from local, seasonal, and organic ingredients. Her inspiration? The food of her childhood, which conjures up memories and feelings. Don't even think about coming to Tokyo without stopping to eat here.

EATRIP
6-31-10 JINGUMAE
SHIBUYA-KU TOKYO, 1F

東京都渋谷区神宮前6-31-10

Reservation required
+81 3-3409-4002
shibuya@mail.com

restaurant-eatrip.com

- YURI NOMURA -

CHEF OF EMOTIONS

Fascinated by the connection between what we feel and what we eat, Yuri is setting out to create a 'laboratory of emotions'. An irresistible encounter.

What were you like as a child?

I was a real foodie. My mother ran a cooking school, so I've always been surrounded by people who loved to eat. And while it's true that I've always been interested in cooking, I never thought I'd make it my profession. I saw cooking as a 'girlie thing'. And I preferred 'boys' talk'! Then I went to study in England and when I came back, I found myself wanting to start cooking.

What are your influences?

First of all, sharing: when you work side-by-side, you create a community, and that's what gives us strength. For me, cooking is the best way to meet people I love, who love the same things as I do. And, finally, home cooking.

What does cooking mean to you?

It means cooking from the heart – it doesn't need to be anything elaborate. This is going to be a place for culinary performances that evoke emotions and memories through the flavors of the dishes.

What's your favorite childhood dish?

A mimosa cake my mother used to make for guests. She always kept some in the fridge for the many visitors who stopped by. And over the course of the day, I would sneak a little piece here, a little piece there ...

What's the typical childhood dish in Japan?

Miso soup!

I'm going to open a laboratory of emotions soon

JONATHAN SAFRAN FOER
電車男

#05

SPEND A NIGHT ON **A LIBRARY BOOKSHELF**

Nothing beats falling asleep while doing what you love most in the world. For the architects Makoto Tanijiri and Ai Yoshida, that means reading. On the 8th floor of an office building, they've created a library with tiny encapsulated rooms where you can spend the night or simply doze off for an afternoon nap.

Just choose a book – a manga or a travel or adventure novel in English or Japanese – slip into your bunk, and pull the curtain shut.

BOOK AND BED TOKYO
1-17-7, NISHI IKEBUKURO, TOSHIMA-KU,
LUMIERE BUILLDING 7F

東京都豊島区西池袋1-17-7 ルミエールビル7階

Prices start at 5,000 yen for the night
Day stays are 500 yen per hour

bookandbedtokyo.com/en/tokyo/index

* beds are not available during the day

GO
CHIP KIDD
AKIRA
AKIRA
AKIRA
AKIRA
鹿児島は
豊かである!

LUTELLA

#06

FRANÇOIS SIMON'S **FAVORITE SUSHI**

We would never have heard of this sushi place if it weren't for the great French food critic, François Simon (the inspiration behind Anton Ego in the animated film, *Ratatouille*), who manages to unearth hidden gastronomic gems around the world. He dug this particular one up in the district of Omote-sando, on the ground floor of an office building.

Makoto, the owner, has been expertly wielding a knife for 50 years: he rolled sushi in restaurants all over Tokyo before opening this discreetly charming spot with its cheerful team. Enter and ask for omakase, which means 'I'll leave it up to you,' and give the sushi master carte blanche. Then watch as a parade of sushi, sashimi, and grilled fish (sardines, sole, octopus, shrimp, tuna...) appears before your eyes – a total of 12 to 15 pieces of incomparable goodness and delicacy.

KIDOGUCHI SUSHI
5-6-3 MINAMIAOYAMA
MINATO TOKYO, B1F

東京都港区南青山5-6-3 メゾン
ブランシュ半地下

+81 3-5467-3992
Reservation required

Lunch 3,000 yen
Dinner 20,000 yen

- FRANÇOIS SIMON -

FOOD CRITIC

François Simon is the undercover food critic of Paris. Everyone knows him, but no one has ever seen him; he tests restaurants surreptitiously. An incurable Nipponophile who has traveled to Japan repeatedly, he knows Tokyo like the back of his hand.

What fascinates you about Japan?

Japan has taught me how to be innocent again. I've been coming here for 25 years, and I realized that I was starting to form a much too precise opinion of this country. I was basically waiting for people to ask me, 'Hey, what do you think about Japan?' Because I had an answer for everything. And then I realized that I actually don't know anything anymore. I've forgotten everything and find myself approaching things like a child again, with just my eyes and memories, without my intellect butting in and imposing structure on it all.

The easier thing are, the less I know and that makes me feel comfortable

What's the flavor of Japan?

Japan tastes like a grain

What's interesting about a grain of rice is isolating the soft heart from the shell when you bite into it.

Last time you came to Japan, you went...

... to Sapporo. I was originally supposed to try out a fancy restaurant, but I told my buddy that I wanted to get to know the real Sapporo. So he took me to a bohemian restaurant, a sort of merry student mess, a bit dusty, where we drank sake and chewed the fat in every language. For me, that's how you get to 'the heart of a grain of rice'.

What approach to traveling do you recommend?

There are two mountains you should try to cross – those of prejudice and comfort. Because, on the other side of those mountains, you'll discover an amazing reward waiting for you: you'll find there's everything to discover. For example, going for onigiri at 7-Eleven at two o'clock in the morning, taking small, slow provincial trains rather than the Shinkansen bullet train, picking up a bento box at the station and eating it on the train while watching the landscape roll by, staying in youth hostels, going to unfamiliar neighborhoods, to museums no one else goes to... In short, making yourself do things that are outside your comfort zone but that teach you something new.

You feel very small, so you keep your mouth shut and taste in Japan, in silence

Get away from what you are and let Japan pervade you

#07

A TRADITIONAL JAPANESE BATH SURROUNED BY PLANTS

Okada-yu, commonly referred to as the 'botanical sentō' (public bath) because of the many plants that beautify the space, is perfect for experiencing a traditional Japanese bath.

Run by the third generation of the same family, it offers several types of bath: jet massage, hinoki (Japanese cypress) wood bath, cold bath, nanobubble bath (which leaves the skin feeling incredibly soft), sauna, hammam and an outdoor bath for men.

The relaxation area includes a large, pleasant library and a small bar.

OKADA-YU
3-43-2 SEKIBARA
ADACHI CITY

東京都足立区関原3-43-2

+81 3-3886-3444

okadayu.com

ONSEN
USER'S GUIDE

Hot baths are a Japanese obsession. Before or after the evening meal, to 'clean the soul', Japanese families head to an onsen (open-air hot spring) or sento (neighborhood public bath). There are baths for women and baths for men. Everyone carries their own bath bucket and a rolled towel on their forehead to protect their hair and keep their head cool.

Get undressed:

wearing a bathing suit is prohibited

(as is having a tattoo)

Your only accessory:

a micro-towel for your head

Head to the showers

Grab a bath bucket

Take a seat on a little bench

and wash yourself thoroughly

Sink into the bath

Caution: the water is very hot – around 107°F, sometimes more

© PAOLO STA. BARBARA

#08

THE MICHELIN-STARRED CHEF **WHO DOES THINGS LIKE NO ONE ELSE**

Den is the only Michelin-starred chef with a sense of humor. If you ask his fellow star-winning colleague Alain Passard of L'Arpège in Paris for his favorite restaurant in Tokyo, he'll immediately slip you this address under the table. Den's restaurant is considered one of the 50 best in the world. Each of his dishes features some incredible sleight of hand that invariably makes his customers laugh. An emoji carved into a carrot, an ant hidden in a salad on purpose ... A sense of humor this great requires great seriousness. His obsession: to reboot young people's idea of traditional Japanese cuisine. And it's working.

JIMBOCHO DEN
2-3-18 JINGUMAE, SHIBUYA-KU
ARCHITECT HOUSE HALL JIA

東京都渋谷区神宮前2-3-18 建築家会館JIA館

+81 3-6455-5433
Reservation required

jimbochoden.com

- DEN -

MICHELIN-STARRED

Where did you pick up this surprising way of cooking?

From my mother, who was a geisha. She taught me how to cook, but above all the art of entertaining your customers. I never went to cooking school, but I did my first apprenticeship in her ryotei (a restaurant run by geishas). The customers, who were in cahoots with her, would constantly send my dishes back to the kitchen to teach me humility. It made me understand that I shouldn't think about myself when I cook, but about my customers. Because if I think about them first, they'll do the same for me.

My mother was a geisha

What kinds of dishes do you cook?

I don't know how to cook anything but traditional Japanese cuisine. Yet I've noticed that young people tend not to eat it anymore; there are too many rules. I thought that was a shame, so I decided to make it fashionable again by making it fun, by getting rid of the taboos.

For me, cooking should be a language, a memory I share

with my customers, whom I don't consider customers so much as friends. When they're in my restaurant, I want them to feel like they're in my home. As it happens, I often personalize my dishes with a drawing, image, or name – something I know about my customer.

How do you come up with your dishes?

We talk about things a lot as a team and compose dishes together, based on our mood at the time. For example, since it isn't customary to have coffee after dessert in Japan, I appropriated a Starbucks mug to make a dessert with a totally unexpected cappuccino–truffle flavor. Since I lost a Michelin star last year, I wrote Starbacks in the hope of winning back a star! Every dish is a story. As far as the ant in the salad is concerned, I put it there on purpose since it's reminiscent of the food our Japanese ancestors ate.

What's the best advice you've ever been given?

The only constant in life is change. That's advice from my mother – I think about it every time I cook. She's 59 years old now. And she's still a geisha!

PHOTO CREDIT: CITY FOODSTERS

#09

1233 SHADES **OF PAPER**

Founded in 1904, this is a 10-story temple to paper: over 1,000 different colors, available as paper, envelopes, origami paper, notebooks, greeting cards, giftwrap (the famous Japanese washi), postcards, and 1,200 types of pens of all dimensions and tip sizes. Incidentally, the colors here aren't numbered but have unusual names instead: sheep skin, little mermaid...

Artists, writers, and designers all flock here for supplies. As for us, we left with 17 pens, almost 7 pounds of paper, and 5 notebooks to fill.

Our two favorite floors:
The 2nd, 'Letters', which is dedicated to snail mail and even has stamps and a mailbox.
The 10th, 'Farm', where you'll find a vegetable garden with incredibly fresh lettuce, which will go on to be harvested and served in the restaurant directly upstairs.

ITOYA
2-7-15 GINZA, CHUO-KU

東京都中央区銀座2-7-15

+81 3-3561-8311

ito-ya.co.jp

P270
P280
P390
P400
P520
P510
P640

ITOYA

#10

HAVE LUNCH IN **A JAPANESE GARDEN**

If you're crazy about tofu, come satisfy your tofu cravings at Tofuya Ukai, a traditional house with Japanese gardens inspired by the Edo period. Here even the waitresses wear hakama, the 'working girl's kimono', with pleated pants that make it easier for them to walk.

The tofu, which is prepared in-house, is offered up in all its forms: age-dengaku (fried over charcoal and basted with sweet-savory miso sauce), tosui-tofu (mixed with soymilk and served in a ceramic bowl), and yuba (tofu skin, a Kyoto specialty).

Take a seat on the tatamis looking out onto the magnificent Japanese gardens, watch the sliding doors close, and let the long procession of dishes begin.

TOFUYA UKAI
4-4-13 SHIBA-KOEN, MINATO-KU

東京都港区芝公園4-4-13

+81 3-3436-1028
Reservation required

ukai.co.jp/english/shiba

WHAT IS THE EDO PERIOD?

The Edo was a key period in the cultural construction of Japan because it was the era (between 1603 and 1868) during which the country closed itself off to foreign influences and developed its local culture. As a result, most of the artisanal crafts associated with traditional Japanese culture today have their roots in the Edo period.

TOFUYA UKAI

JAZZ
JAZZ
JAZZ
JAZZ
BLUE NOTE

THE WORLD'S **BIGGEST BOOKSTORE**

A 180-foot-long 'magazine street' that runs across three gigantic buildings. The Tsutaya Daikanyama bookstore, considered one of the 20 most beautiful bookstores in the world, is a magazine lover's temple, a six-floor modern maze of everything that exists in terms of reading material, both Japanese and international: literature, cooking, travel, cars, art, architecture, music ... And it's open until 2am. Pretty mind-blowing.

TIP: Don't forget to go up to the 1st floor of the main building, where you'll find the bookshop Anjin. You can lounge on enormous sofas and have a drink while browsing one of the 30,000 vintage magazines rounded up from antique shops around the world.

TSUTAYA
16-15 SARUGAKUCHO,
SHIBUYA-KU

東京都渋谷区猿楽町16-15

+81 3-3770-2525

real.tsite.jp/daikanyama/english/index.html

#12

THE WORLD'S **SMALLEST BOOKSTORE**

A single room with a single book: that's the rule for this micro-bookstore, which is a perfect example of Japanese-style minimalism. A new book is chosen every week – a new universe, really, since the entire room is tailored to the featured book. You can buy the book, but also meet its author and see objects associated with it.

MORIOKA SHOTEN & CO
1-28-15 GINZA, CHUO-KU,
1F SUZUKI BUILDING

東京都中央区銀座
1−28−15 鈴木ビル 1F

+81 3-3535-5020

#13

MAGIC,
PURE AND SIMPLE

In an alley in the Ginza district, a door opens onto a small, completely black room with a large table and eight chairs. You enter and sit down. Silence. First, mysterious sounds, then a bamboo forest appears on the walls, flowers begin to grow, butterflies flutter. A shower of petals rains down on your table, which turns into a river as a butterfly takes off from your plate.

You're at Tokyo's MoonFlower Sagaya Ginza, Art by teamLab. There aren't many such digital restaurants in the world, and this is the most accessible. It's expensive, yes, but so incredibly beautiful, magical, and delicious that it's worth traveling across the entire world just to come here.

MOONFLOWER SAGAYA GINZA, ART BY TEAMLAB
2-5-19 GINZA, CHUO-KU, 6F, PUZZLE GINZA

東京都中央区銀座 2-5-19
PUZZLE 銀座 6F

+81 3-6263-2525
Reservation required

moonflower-sagaya.com

MOONFLOWER SAGAYA GINZA,
ART BY TEAMLAB

#14

CELEBRATE YOUR **'UN-BIRTHDAY'**

On a busy street in the Shibuya district, two restaurants face each other. In one of them, the customers are all men; in the other, all women. In the men's restaurant, you eat fish in peace and quiet; in the women's, skewers are served amidst singing. Two types of food, two different atmospheres that taunt each other, each trying to outdo the other in the number of customers they can pull in from the street. We chose our team – the women's, which holds the trump card: celebrating birthdays like you've never seen before.

TIP: Call ahead, tell them it's the birthday of one of your fellow diners... We won't tell you what happens next.

TEPPEN ONNA DOJO
41-23 UDAGAWA-CHO,
SHIBUYA

東京都渋谷区宇田川町
41-23　第二大久保ビル1F

+81 3-5428-3698
Reservation recommended

Prices start at 2,000 yen

15

A TIMELESS **MUSIC BAR**

A passion for vinyl records, a commitment to collecting them and a desire to share them with others: these are the ingredients that make Tokyo a mecca of music bars – and Grandfather's is the best example.

You'll quickly lose all sense of time in this little tavern in the basement of a building in Shibuya: the subdued lighting, the drinks, the music ... Wait, what year is it again?

Behind the bar, Mr Ishikawa, elegant and meticulous, selects one of his 2,000 rock, soul and funk records to put on the turntable. The rule is simple: play just one song from the record before switching to another. And that's how it's been since 1971.

GRANDFATHER'S BAR
B1F FLAT BLDG, 1-24-7 SHIBUYA, SHIBUYA-KU

東京都渋谷区渋谷1-24-7渋谷フラットビルB1

+81 3-3407-9505

grandfather.jp/shibuya
info@grandfather.jp

‘JAPANESEISMS’

There are certain words that exist only in Japanese because you can only perceive the state of being, mood, or feeling they describe through the lens of Japanese culture. Here, we've selected our six favorite ‘Japaneseisms’ for you.

Komorebi

木漏れ日

---

*SUN RAYS

Sunlight filtering through the leaves of a tree.

Shinrinyoku

森林浴

*FOREST BATH

Taking a forest bath means going for a walk deep in the woods where there's nothing but silence, peace and relaxation.

Yuugen

幽幻

*THE BEAUTY OF A PLACE

Perceiving the universe in a way that unleashes emotions that are too deep and mysterious to express in words..

Shoganai

しょうがない

*THE VICISSITUDES OF LIFE

'There's nothing you can do, that's just how it is'. Accepting that something is out of your control in any event and that you need to keep going without regret.

Hijiame

肘雨

*ELBOW RAIN

In Japan, there are 50 different expressions for rain, but our favorite is elbow rain: a shower so sudden that you don't even have time to get out your umbrella and have to cover yourself with your elbows.

Wabisabi

わびさび

*BEAUTY OF TIME PASSING

It's imperfect, ephemeral, worn with age? That's precisely what makes it beautiful. This esthetic of time passing is known as wabisabi.

SOSAIBOU
4-1-9 MEGURO-HONCHO,
MEGURO-KU

東京都目黒区目黒本町4-1-9

+81 3-3710-4336
Reservation required

Menu starting at
7,000 yen

#16

HAVE DINNER **AT THE OLD FOLKS'**

What is this anyway? Their living room? Kitchen? Restaurant? One thing is for sure: Katsuro and Mieko are the owners of Sosaibou. He's the poet, serving up dishes that seem like they've been conjured up by magic; she's the party animal, pouring the sake. They must be at least 80 years old and can't live without each other: two diminutive eccentrics who've been serving 'zen' cuisine, inspired by monks, for 33 years.

Their dishes combine every possible color, shape, and flavor. For Katsuro, it's a metaphor for the medley of life: some things are bitter, some sweet – and you simply have to accept it.

A place of joy, wisdom, and ... inebriation.

WHAT IS ZEN CUISINE?

In Japan, it's called shojin ryori: the cuisine of the monks, an 800-year-old philosophy inspired by the seasons and prepared without meat or fish... and without onions, leeks, garlic, or other root vegetables, since harvesting them means killing them.

TOKYO,
5AM IN THE MORNING

#17

GO ON A **BIKE RIDE IN TOKYO**

Yanaka is Tokyo's oldest neighborhood, one of the rare areas that has preserved its temples, wood houses, and peaceful alleyways, which resound with the gentle clattering of bicycles ... Speaking of: do like the locals and go for a ride around Yanaka on a bike, which you can rent from tokyobike. This design boutique, which doubles as a coffee and lifestyle shop, is dedicated to bicycle lovers, of which there are many in Japan – devotees who take their bikes with them everywhere: on the subway and to the office, even going so far as to sleep with them. As you can see from the hipster Instagram account @tokyobike_jp, which is dedicated entirely to these pedal-powered two-wheelers.

TOKYOBIKE
4-2-39 YANAKA, TAITŌ

東京都台東区谷中4-2-39

+81 3-5809-0980

tokyobikerentals.com

TOKYOBIKE

HALVA
BOSPHORE

ときわ
三喜鮨
鮨
Asahi
大 ASAHI BEER 20
2-9

FIVE THINGS TO DO BY BIKE IN YANAKA

- meditate in the zen gardens of the Nezu-jinja Shrine, a traditional Shinto sanctuary
- visit SCAI THE BATHHOUSE, a contemporary art gallery located in a former onsen
- discover the underside of umbrellas and other design objects at the KONCENT boutique in Kuramae
- taste and buy tea at Nakamura Tea Life Store, a traditional teahouse
- create your own personalized planner or ideal color of ink at the stationery store Kakimori

#18

DRINK YUZU JUICE **AT THE NEZU MUSEUM**

It's the little pleasures that add spice to the day. For example: stealing off to the Nezu Museum in Minato, slipping past the bamboo screen, following the pebble pathway, buying your ticket to this museum dedicated to traditional Japanese arts and crafts, passing through the exhibition rooms, opening the door to the Nezu Café, taking a seat at a table overlooking the lush Japanese gardens, ordering a glass of yuzu juice, pressing your face against the window and... simply savoring the moment.

NEZU MUSEUM
6-5-1 MINAMI-AOYAMA,
MINATO-KU, TOKYO

東京都港区南青山6-5-1

+81 3-3400-2536

You must purchade a ticket
to the Nezu Museum
to enter the café

のんべい横
2F

みや

#19

MINI-STREET **MAXI-BENDER**

No, not that one – the other one. Because, yes, you'll definitely hear everyone talking about the famous Golden Gai, the working-class neighborhood teeming with bars that's more commonly known as the 'neighborhood of thirst'. As for us, what we're talking about is 'drunkards' lane', right behind the train tracks of Shibuya, which you'll find thanks to the rows of lanterns hanging over the entrance. Behind them lies an alleyway full of tiny bars that serve sake. Our favorite: the one at the end of the street, spattered with graffiti, which you access via a miniscule staircase. It only has room for four customers, but also offers karaoke. Just ask the boss – he likes to sing too. Prepare to leave lurching, but in very high spirits.

SHIBUYA NONBEI YOKOCHO
1-25 SHIBUYA, SHIBUYA-KU

東京都渋谷区渋谷一丁目25

Go here after dinner

#20

A BREAK FROM THE HUSTLE AND BUSTLE OF CITY LIFE

Go fishing in the middle of a metropolis of 14 million inhabitants? In Tokyo, you can – and the Ichigaya Fish Center is probably one of the best places in the Japanese capital to indulge in a moment of peace and quiet as you taunt the fish. Tucked away between skyscrapers and railroad tracks, it has been offering Tokyoites a break from the hustle and bustle of city life since 1950.

There are two pools: a large one for experts and a smaller one for children and beginners. Fishing sessions are charged by the hour, but N.B: the fish must be released again. The point is not to catch your next meal, but to relax and soak up the atmosphere of the place.

ICHIGAYA FISH CENTER
1-CHŌME-1 ICHIGAYATAMACHI,
SHINJUKU CITY

東京都新宿区市谷田町１－１

ichigaya-fc.com

#21

SPEND A FEW HOURS IN **A LOVE HOTEL**

You've met someone special on the streets of Tokyo, but your hotel is too far away? Created in the 1950s, when the size of apartments didn't give the Japanese the necessary privacy at home, Love Hotels are the perfect solution: there are hundreds of them in the city, for every taste and need, and, as their name suggests, you go there to make love.

Today, almost every Love Hotel offers an automated check-in for greater discretion, you'll find all kinds of sex toys, and many of the rooms have themes so you can live out your fantasies: class-room, Santa Claus, UFO, etc.

Stay just for a few hours or spend the whole night.

LOVE HOTELS

More information and a selection of Love Hotels is available at matcha-jp.com/en/12470

#22

SPEND A NIGHT **IN OLD TOKYO**

... and wake up on a tatami mat. Greet your neighbors and ride a bike through the district's small alleyways. Hanare – a guest house-cum-hotel-cum-traditional inn located in the peaceful Yanaka district – offers total immersion in the local life.

A stay at Hanare is basically a stay in the neighborhood: you get to experience the same places as the locals. So you might wake up in a room at one end of the street and grab breakfast at the other, before going to the sento (public baths) on another street. In the evening, slip on geta (those famous Japanese wooden flip-flop clogs), enter your completely empty room, and unroll your futon and duvet on the tatami mats. Lights out: good night!

HANARE
HAGISO, 3-10-25 YANAKA, TAITO-KU

東京都台東区谷中3-10-25
HAGISO

+81 3-5834-7301
hanare.hagiso.jp/en

About 20,000 yen for a room

#23

LISTEN TO CLASSICAL MUSIC IN **A BAR FROM THE 1950s**

The Lion Café is one of Tokyo's most magical offbeat places, located in the midst of the chaos and sex shops of Shibuya. People come here to listen to classical music in a truly timeless atmosphere, sipping coffee or strawberry milk in front of a bust of Beethoven and wooden speakers that are almost 3 metres high. A true gem.

To make the most of this exceptional ambience, follow the lead of the other customers: close your eyes, listen and enjoy.

Originally opened in 1923, the Lion Café (officially Meikyoku Lion Café – *meikyoku* means masterpiece) – was rebuilt in 1950, after the war, when having a hi-fi system at home was still an unheard-of luxury. To unwind and listen to music, people went to specialized cafés, of which the Lion is one of the last remaining examples.

LION CAFÉ
2 CHOME-19-13 DOGENZAKA
SHIBUYA CITY

東京都渋谷区道玄坂2-19-13

+81 3-3461-6858

lion.main.jp

#24

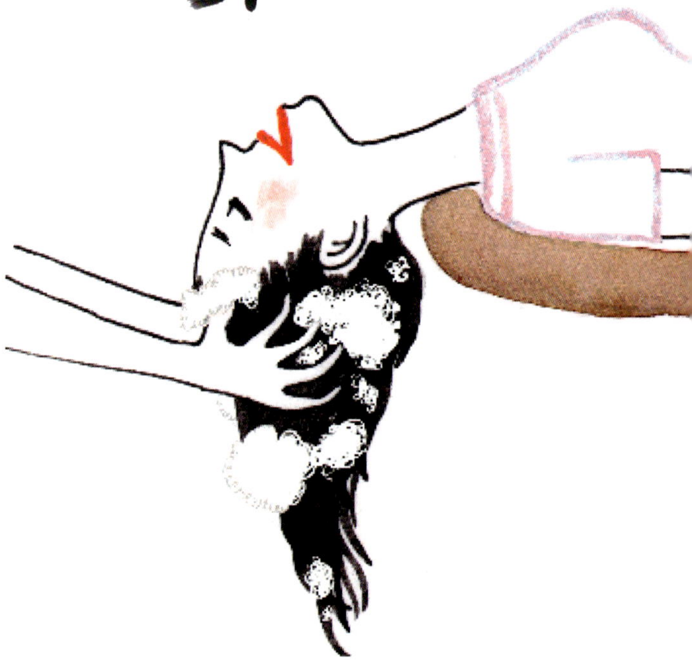

TREAT YOURSELF **TO A HEAD SPA**

3 BEAUTY SALONS

Head massages are a ritual the Japanese indulge in regularly to unwind after a long day. Where? At head spas, which specialize in hair and head care. We've picked out three for you, to ensure that you get a head massage that's truly out of this world.

> THE MOST HEAVENLY:

It's ridiculous – literally, since this bohemian hair salon located in a small apartment is actually called Ridicule, French for ridiculous. The house specialty: the head spa, a divinely delicious head massage.

RIDICULE
3-31-13 JINGUMAE,
SHIBUYA-KU

東京都渋谷区神宮前3-31-13

+81 3-3478-7332
Reservation required

ridicule.jp

> THE MOST TRANSCENDENTAL:

It's a bit far to get to (45 minutes from downtown Tokyo), but it's absolutely worth it. At this hair spa, they'll wash, massage, and do your hair while you lie cradled in a cocoon-like hammock.

COCONA
3-16-1 KOENJI-KITA, SUGINAMI-KU, 2F,3F

東京都杉並区高円寺北3-16-1
田中ビル2.3階

+81 3-5356-6543
Reservation required

salon-cocona.com

> THE MOST TARGETED:

At Uka, they start by giving you a detailed hair-and-scalp diagnosis before bringing you to a private room to minister exclusively to you. Depending on the time of day, you can choose shampoo with chamomile, lavender, and rosemary extracts to put you to sleep ('Nighty night!') or with peppermint for an energizing boost ('Wake up!'). Then they wash your hair, massaging the pressure points on your scalp and at the base of your neck with alternatingly firm and gentle gestures. Finally, they wrap up your hair in a heated towel before styling or blow-drying it. You'll emerge 45 minutes later, feeling relaxed from toe to head.

UKA TOKYO MIDTOWN
TOKYO GALLERIA 2F
9-7-4 AKASAKA, MINATO-KU

東京都港区赤坂9-7-4 東京ミッドタウン ガレリア2F

+81 3-5413-7236
Reservation required

uka.co.jp/salons/midtown

COCONA HAIRDRESSER

#25

'APPLY' TO **A RESTAURANT**

This is a restaurant you have to earn: to eat at Bohemian, you must send a 'cover letter' or know someone who knows someone who knows someone ... It makes sense, though: there are only two tables in the entire place, and Kazu, the chef, is a gastronomic visionary. He's already been to Burning Man and is obsessed with cooking in the craziest places in the world.

Seasonal fish, bell peppers, corn, shellfish, mushrooms, brochettes... Kazu prepares everything over a fire, according to the traditional method used by the fishermen of Hokkaido, who used to cook on their boats. So take a seat at the irori, the traditional table with an opening in the middle for the fire, massaging your bare feet on little round pellets, and let the ceremony begin.

Listen, we'll even give you a little leg up... Here's where you should send your cover letter: kazu@playearth.jp

BOHEMIAN SECRET

Send an application email to: kazu@playearth.jp

#26

EAT
THE BEST SANDWICH OF YOUR LIFE

It's the most expensive sandwich in Tokyo, but you'll remember it for a lifetime. Welcome to the Wagyumafia club!

Here, they offer wagyu sandwiches, made with Japanese beef (among the best in the world), which melts in the mouth like caramel. Cut into cubes for a captivating presentation, the meat is coated in panko breadcrumbs and served with a secret sauce.

Framed between two slices of Japanese brioche bread, it will look at you from the top of its throne because it knows that you will not forget it!

WAGYUMAFIA
THE CUTLET SANDWICH
1 CHOME-26-1-108 KAMIMEGURO,
MEGURO-KU

東京都目黒区上目黒1-26-1
中目黒アトラスタワー 1F

exploretock.com/wagyumafiathecutletsandwich

'RENÉ MAGRITTE DINNER FOR DELVAUX' 2015
© MASAYUKI SAITO

#27

EAT **ART**

You don't know the address or who you'll be with. In fact, up until the last minute, you have no idea what's about to happen. All you do know is that it's going to be a truly memorable night. The mysterious Ayako Suwa is a performance artist who organizes guerilla restaurants in Tokyo at which guests are party to extraordinary culinary experiences. Like nothing you've ever eaten before.

But – we're leaving it up to you to figure out how to get yourself put on the list of potential guests.

FOOD CREATION

foodcreation.jp/en

'TASTE OF PHOTOGRAPHY' 2015
@ NAOHIRO UDAGAWA

'TASTE OF LUNASOL' 2015
@ LUNASOL

- AYAKO SUWA -

CULINARY ARTIST

PHOTO CREDIT: ITTETSU MATSUOKA

The artist Ayako Suwa has worked for Dior, Agnès B, contemporary museums, and big-name chefs. Her obsession: retranscribing the taste of emotions into flavors. She has created the taste of anxiety blended slowly with that of terror, guilt, pride, melancholy ... Ayako turns cooking into a profound life experience.

When was this desire of yours for a guerilla restaurant born?

When I was four years old. I grew up in nature, which simultaneously terrified and attracted me. Jellyfish in the sea, insects in flowers – everything fascinated me. So I decided to organize a guerilla restaurant: I prepared a tea party with dead insects, pollen, and flowers, and invited kids who were younger than me and ate it all without knowing what it was.

We eat to live, taste to grow

What fuels your inspiration?

Desire, curiosity, and the urge to eat. When I see people on the street, I like to ask myself what they eat, how they live, and so on.

What's your most recent discovery?

It was in the sea: some strangely shaped seaweed I'd never seen before. In fact, what I look for in food isn't a good taste but the element of surprise.

How does a guerilla restaurant work?

From the moment guests arrive, they're plunged into a special universe. Starting from when they sit down at the table, they have to respect certain rules. Namely, they must:

- keep their eyes closed;
- eat with their hands;
- consume each offering i single mouthful; and
- do so at the same time as the other guests. To share in the same sensation.

How do you conceive of your guerilla restaurants upstream?

I think of them as a bit like ceremonies. My waiters are artists to whom I assign roles, characters even. The question I ask myself each time is: How can I best express the taste of this experience? How can I make a deep impression on my guests to ensure they leave with lasting memories?

I only like to eat bizarre things

'JOURNEY ON THE TABLE WITH VVG TAIPEI' 2012
PHOTO CREDIT: VVG

HOSHINOYA KARUIZAWA,
KITASAKU-GUN, NAGANO, 389-0194

長野県北佐久郡軽井沢町長倉
2148

For exceptional occasions only
since it's very expensive
prices start at 52,000 yen / night

+81 50-3786-1144
Reservation required

hoshinoya.com/karuizawa/en/

#28

SPEND A MAGICAL NIGHT **OUTSIDE OF TOWN**

3 RYOKANS OUTSIDE OF TOKYO

> A LUXURY RYOKAN

For just one night, leave the Tokyo crowds behind for this dreamlike spot straight out of a Miyazaki movie: the Hoshinoya Karuizawa resort, a large ryokan with a peaceful onsen, stone paths, and small wooden pagodas all clustered around a lake in the middle of the woods. At nightfall, a boat glides beneath your window to light the dozens of floating lanterns that shimmer in the dark like fireflies. There's a private onsen in each pagoda, but you can also climb up to the Meditation Bath, hot baths in a room with shoji screen walls.

1 hour outside of Tokyo by bullet train

WHAT'S A RYOKAN?

A ryokan is a traditional Japanese inn, built using typical materials (wood, bamboo, rice paper, tatami mats) and with minimalist furnishings (low tables, sliding partitions, futons). You move them aside at the end of the day since the rooms serve as both bedrooms and living rooms. Though there aren't many ryokans in Tokyo, there are a lot more in Kyoto and in the Japanese countryside.

HOSHINOYA KARUIZAWA

> A PRIVATE BATH IN THE MOUNTAINS

With its panoramic bedroom views of the sea, the Kazekomichi ryokan is located in the city of Atami with its magnificent palm trees and coastline. The best time of day to enjoy the view: in the morning, looking out from your private hot bath on the terrace as the sun rises over the sea.

30 minutes outside of Tokyo by bullet train

WATEI-KAZEKOMICHI
28-18 BAIEN-CHO, ATAMI, SHIZUOKA

静岡県熱海市梅園町28-18

Prices start at 38,000 yen / night for two people

contact@kazekomichi.jp

kazekomichi.jp/en/

THE DISCREET CHARM OF THE SHINKANSEN

The landscapes are so beautiful in Japan that the experience of journeying by train can be just as important as the destination. To get out of Tokyo, you can take small provincial trains or, to save time, the shinkansen bullet train.
Before getting on the train at Tokyo station, choose a take-out bento box at Ekibenya Matsuri (in the station's main hall) and savor it as you watch the landscape slide by.

> JAPAN'S BEST ONSEN

Located in the city of Kusatsu, the Kusatsu Onsen was voted Japan's best, above all for the therapeutic quality of its water, but also for the beauty of its hot springs, which intersect right in the middle of the city, forming little rivers. Spend the day here and then sleep at the Boun Hotel.

About two and a half hours from Tokyo by bullet + local train

KUSATSU ONSEN BOUN
433-1 KUSATSU-MACHI,
AGATSUMA-GUN, GUNMA

群馬県吾妻郡草津町433-1

Prices start at 30,000 yen / night for two people	+81 279-88-3251	hotelboun.com

© 9HOURS

#29

STAY AT A **CAPSULE HOTEL**

Tokyo is teeming with capsule hotels, which are designed to optimize space by offering rows of stacked and side-by-side sleeping pods instead of rooms. Claustrophobics beware! Our personal favorite is the Nine Hours, where customers stay for precisely that long: enough time to sleep – and maybe even then some. It looks like an intergalactic space station and offers all the classiness and technology we love so much about Japan: sunrise alarm-clocks and ergonomic pillows; pajamas and slippers provided.

9HOURS
3F-8F 1-4-15 HYAKUNINCHO
SHINJUKU-KU, 169-0073

東京都新宿区百人町1-4-15 ナインアワーズ北新宿ビル3-8F

Prices start at 5,000 yen / night	+81 3-5291-7337	ninehours.co.jp/en

#30

THE CRAZIEST **MUSEUM**

We've already mentioned one of teamLab's creations, but they've struck again at the eleventh hour – and there's no way we were going to leave out their latest crazy project. This time, they've opened the Mori Building Digital Art, a truly one-of-a-kind museum where visitors will never see the same thing twice. Why? Because the works here are 'alive' and react directly to contact with viewers, with the help of some 500 projectors and computers. Here, a waterfall plunges down a wall; there, you wander through a forest of lamps or along the edge of a virtual rice paddy. The goal? To show that the world has no limits. Mission accomplished.

MORI Building DIGITAL ART MUSEUM: teamLab Borderless
ODAIBA PALETTE TOWN, 1-3-8 AOMI, KOTO-KU

東京都江東区青海1-3-8 お台場パレットタウン

+81 3-6406-3949

teamlab.art/e/borderless-azabudai

MORI BUILDING DIGITAL ART MUSEUM: TEAMLAB BORDERLESS

MANY THANKS TO

AURÉLIE R, for being the first to introduce Fany to Tokyo.
IKUMI, for accompanying her on all her explorations and for the 1,001 incredible strings she pulled for us.
IWONKA, for ferreting out priceless spots, investigating unheard-of places, managing to fit 'round pegs in square holes,' and for all the sake-fueled belly laughs.
AKO, for introducing us to so many amazing people and for translating the craziest conversations.
OUSSAMA, or getting up to no good with us in Japan.
KANAKO, AURÉLIE S AND FABIAN, for retranscribing the soul of this city in pictures and drawings.
THOMAS, our expedition leader.

This book was created by:

Fany and Amandine Péchiodat,
co-founders of My Little Paris, authors

Iwonka Bancerek, local scout and blogger,
follow her on Instragram on @toteone

Kanako Kuno, illustrator

Fabian Parkes, photographer

Aurélie Saint-Martin, artistic director and layout design

Emmanuelle Willard Toulemonde, layout

Sophie Schlondorff, translation

Jana Gough, editing

Eleni Salemi, proofreading

Clémence Mathé and Morgane De Wulf, publishing

Cover: © Astemir Almov – Unsplash

You can write to us at info@editionsjonglez.com
Follow us on Instagram on @jonglez_publishing

From the same publisher

Atlases

Atlas of extreme weather
Atlas of forbidden places
Atlas of geographical curiosities
Atlas of unusual wines

Photo books

Abandoned America
Abandoned Asylums
Abandoned Australia
Abandoned Belgium
Abandoned Churches: Unclaimed places of worship
Abandoned cinemas of the world
Abandoned France
Abandoned Germany
Abandoned Italy
Abandoned Japan
Abandoned Lebanon
Abandoned Spain
Abandoned USSR
Abandoned world – An AI-generated exploration
After the Final Curtain – The Fall of the American Movie Theater
After the Final Curtain – America's Abandoned Theaters
Baikonur – Vestiges of the Soviet space programme
Cinemas – A French heritage
Clickbait – A visual journey through AI-generated stories
Destination wellness – The 35 best places in the world to take time out
Forbidden France
Forbidden Places – Vol. 1
Forbidden Places – Vol. 2
Forbidden Places – Vol. 3
Forgotten France
Forgotten Heritage
Oblivion
Secret sacred sites
Venice deserted
Venice from the skies

Secret guides

Secret Amsterdam
Secret Bali – An unusual guide
Secret Bangkok
Secret Barcelona
Secret Bath – An unusual guide
Secret Belfast
Secret Berlin
Secret Boston – An unusual guide
Secret Brighton – An unusual guide
Secret Brooklyn
Secret Brussels
Secret Budapest
Secret Buenos Aires
Secret Campania
Secret Cape Town
Secret Copenhagen
Secret Corsica
Secret Dolomites
Secret Dublin – An unusual guide
Secret Edinburgh – An unusual guide
Secret Florence
Secret French Riviera
Secret Geneva
Secret Glasgow
Secret Granada
Secret Helsinki
Secret Johannesburg
Secret Lisbon
Secret Liverpool – An unusual guide
Secret London – An unusual guide
Secret London – Unusual bars & restaurants
Secret Los Angeles – An unusual guide
Secret Louisiana – An unusual guide
Secret Madrid
Secret Mexico City
Secret Milan
Secret Montreal – An unusual guide
Secret Naples
Secret New Orleans
Secret New York – An unusual guide
Secret New York – Curious activities
Secret New York – Hidden bars & restaurants
Secret Normandy
Secret Paris
Secret Prague
Secret Provence
Secret Rio
Secret Rome
Secret Seville
Secret Singapore
Secret Stockholm
Secret Sussex – An unusual guide
Secret Tokyo
Secret Tuscany
Secret Vienna
Secret Washington D.C.
Secret York – An unusual guide

Soul of guides

Soul of Amsterdam
Soul of Athens
Soul of Barcelona
Soul of Berlin
Soul of Brussels
Soul of Kyoto
Soul of Lisbon
Soul of Los Angeles
Soul of Marrakesh
Soul of Marseille
Soul of Milan
Soul of New York
Soul of Paris
Soul of Rome
Soul of Venice

Follow us on Facebook and Instagram

Registration of copyright: February 2025 - Edition: 03
ISBN: 978-2-36195-850-3
Printed in Slovakia by Polygraf